IT'S A FACT! Real-Life Reads

The World of a
VIKING WARRIOR

by Ruth Owen

Series consultant:

Suzy Gazlay, MA
Recipient, Presidential Award for Excellence in Science Teaching

Ruby Tuesday Books

Published in 2015 by Ruby Tuesday Books Ltd.

Copyright © 2015 Ruby Tuesday Books Ltd.

Editor: Mark J. Sachner
Designer: Emma Randall
Production: John Lingham

Photo Credits:
Alamy: 8 (bottom), 15 (bottom), 16, 21 (bottom), 23 (bottom), 26 (bottom), 28–29; Cosmographics: 6, 20, 25 (top), 27 (top); Christer Johansson: 11 (top); Public Domain: 15 (top), 17, 21 (top), 23 (center), 27 (bottom), 29 (top); Shutterstock: Cover, 4–5, 7 (top), 8 (top), 9, 10, 11 (bottom), 12–13, 14 (i4lcocl2), 15 (center), 18–19 (Arne Bramsen), 19 (top), 19 (bottom: De Visu), 24, 25 (bottom), 26 (top); Bjørn Christian Tørrissen: 7 (bottom).

Library of Congress Control Number: 2014920329

ISBN 978-1-909673-90-8

Printed and published in the United States of America

For further information including rights and permissions requests, please contact our Customer Service Department at 877-337-8577.

Contents

Terror from the Sea

In the year 793, terror came to the tiny English island of Lindisfarne. Vikings!

Lindisfarne was home to a **monastery**.
Here, peaceful Christian monks, or holy men, lived and worshiped God. The monastery contained many beautiful and valuable religious objects. It was these treasures that the Vikings desired.

The band of Viking warriors sailed from their icy homeland in the north of Europe. Then they unleashed a brutal attack on the defenseless people of Lindisfarne. They hacked the monks to death. They burned down buildings and stole the treasures.

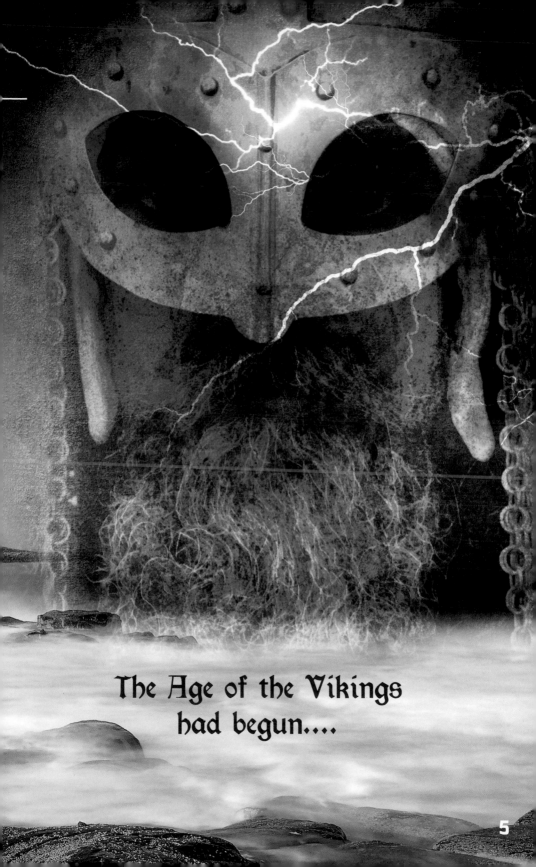

The Age of the Vikings
had begun....

The Norsemen

The Age of the Vikings was a time in history more than 1,000 years ago. It lasted from the late 700s to around the year 1050.

The Vikings came from northern Europe. They were also known as Norsemen, or "people from the North." The Vikings were **hardy** people. They had to survive long, dark, freezing-cold winters.

Vikings lived in small settlements led by chiefs, or noblemen. They were farmers, fishermen, hunters, and trappers. Growing crops and raising animals in the cold north was a tough life, however.

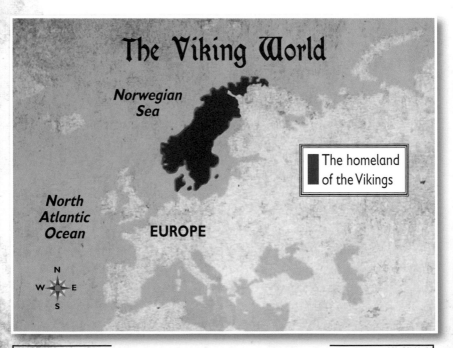

The Vikings lived throughout an area known as Scandinavia. In the modern world, this area is made up of Norway, Sweden, and Denmark.

Vikings built settlements on the coast. In many places they lived on rocky land surrounded by mountains.

In parts of Norway and Sweden it is dark day and night for weeks at a time during winter. Like modern-day Scandinavian people, the Vikings lived through long periods of darkness.

Life in a Viking Village

Viking people built houses from wood or stone. Inside there was usually just one large room. In winter, a family's cows and other animals came inside and shared the house!

Some Viking men were expert carpenters who built ships. Others were smiths who made swords and other weapons from metal. Viking women cooked, milked the cows, made cheese, and baked bread. They also wove wool into cloth and made their families' clothes.

A replica of a Viking house

Viking children did not go to school. They learned about Viking history, gods, and laws from old stories and songs.

In the center of a Viking home there was a fire for cooking. People slept under animal skins and woolen rugs.

Vikings raised cattle, sheep, and goats. They grew wheat, oats, and barley, which were made into bread, porridge, and beer. They also grew cabbages, beans, peas, and onions.

Wild boar

Vikings hunted wild boars, hares, ducks, and deer, including reindeer.

Wild garlic

Mushrooms

Cloudberries

Seagull eggs

Vikings gathered seabird eggs, mushrooms, nuts, berries, and wild garlic.

Sailors and Warriors

Viking men not only farmed, fished, or hunted. They were also skillful sailors and fearsome warriors!

Vikings had fighting in their blood. Their **ancestors** lived in tribes across the north. For centuries these tribes fought each other for land and power. Vikings also had sailing in their blood. Their homeland was surrounded by the sea. They often sailed around the coast to get from place to place. It was easier to travel by water than over the mountains and icy, rocky land.

With adventure and battle in their hearts, the Vikings became raiders. Each summer, once calmer seas and warmer weather arrived, Viking warriors set sail to seek out new lands and riches.

Rock art made by the Vikings' ancestors includes pictures of ships and warriors.

There are many ancient stone monuments in Scandinavia that are shaped like ships. Some stone ships were built as graves. Why others were built is still a mystery.

Fjord

In some parts of the Vikings' homeland deep, narrow waterways, called **fjords**, snaked their way inland from the sea. The Vikings used the fjords to sail from place to place.

Viking Longships

A Viking longship was powered by the wind.
When there was no wind available, the
warriors rowed hard to power their ship.

When sailing on fjords or rivers, a Viking ship
sometimes reached frozen water or another blockage.
Then the crew pulled the huge, heavy ship ashore and
dragged it over land. Once the men had passed the
blockage, they set sail again.

During ocean voyages, the men survived
by eating long-lasting, sundried fish.
They also attacked coastal settlements
to steal food and drink.

This illustration shows
how a Viking ship looked.
It was made from the
wood of oak trees.

Prow of
the ship

The Warriors'
shields

At night, the crew slept on the ship's deck. The men covered the deck with the sail to create a tent. Then they wrapped themselves in waterproof sleeping bags made from seal skins.

The ship's large, square sail was probably woven from sheep's wool.

Oars

A Viking Warrior

By the time he was 16, a young Viking was considered a man.

When he set sail on a raiding voyage, he was armed with a battle-ax or spear. Some wealthy warriors also owned swords. To protect his body in battle, a Viking carried a round, wooden shield.

A Viking's dream was to live and die with honor as a brave warrior. For a Viking, **reputation** was everything. To be remembered as a coward was a Viking warrior's worst nightmare.

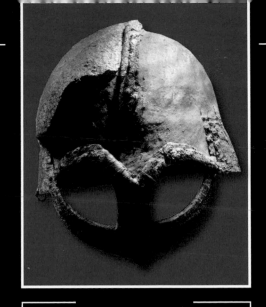

Vikings wore protective helmets made of iron or leather. This iron helmet is from the late 900s. It was found in a Viking grave.

Chainmail

A Viking warrior wore a protective leather tunic. A wealthy man might wear a tunic made of metal chainmail.

A Viking sword from the mid 900s.

A Way of Life and Death

To the people they attacked, Vikings were terrifying.

The men were often big and tall. They were strong, skillful fighters. And they were not afraid of fighting to the death!

Vikings believed that if a warrior died a heroic death in battle, he would be allowed to enter the Viking heaven of Valhalla. Here, a Viking warrior would spend his days fighting with other heroes. Then he would spend the night feasting.

Viking people worshiped many gods. The Vikings' greatest and most important god was Odin. He brought victory in battle. Thor, the god of thunder, was the strongest of all the gods. Many Viking warriors looked to him as their protector.

This painting shows the Viking god Thor. He carried a mighty hammer that could flatten mountains and crush the skulls of giants!

Thor had a girdle, or belt, of might. When he put on this belt, his strength doubled.

Ruthless Raiders

In the early morning darkness, a Viking longship would glide up onto a beach.

Sometimes, Vikings raided coastal villages. At other times, they would descend on a monastery or church filled with valuable objects. Asleep in their beds, the Vikings' victims would have no idea that death and destruction was heading their way.

When the moment was right, the warriors attacked. Sometimes their victims fought back. Then the Vikings did battle with their swords, axes, and spears. At other times, the raiders murdered defenseless men, women, and children.

In the old Norse language the word "Viking" means "a pirate raid." People who went raiding were said to be "going Viking."

Viking raiders stole gold, jewels, money, clothes, food, wine, cattle, tools—anything that was valuable or useful. Loaded with stolen goods, they then rushed back to their ship and made a quick getaway.

A Viking ship often had the head of a dragon or some other fierce creature on its prow. This creature was the spirit of the ship. The Vikings believed it terrified the spirits of the lands they raided.

Slave Traders

Viking warriors attacked settlements around the coast of mainland Europe. They also carried out raids in England, Scotland, and Ireland.

Some Viking longships carried a truly horrific cargo—human beings captured to become slaves. Vikings kept some slaves to work for them. Others were treated as goods to be sold.

In the mid 800s, Vikings built a settlement in Ireland. Today, that settlement is Ireland's capital city, Dublin. The settlement soon became the largest slave market in Europe. Each year, dozens of Viking ships arrived loaded with slaves. Many Vikings became very wealthy buying and selling people.

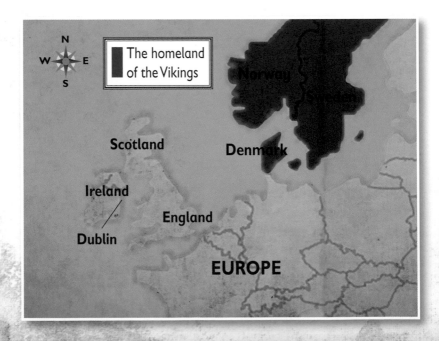

The homeland of the Vikings

Norway
Sweden
Scotland
Denmark
Ireland
England
Dublin
EUROPE

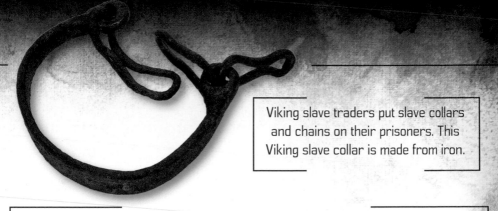

Viking slave traders put slave collars and chains on their prisoners. This Viking slave collar is made from iron.

At the Viking slave market in Dublin, a slave trader could sell a male slave for 12 ounces (340 g) of silver. A female slave could be sold for 8 ounces (227 g) of silver.

This painting shows a Viking slave trader selling a woman to **merchants** from Asia.

Invaders and Settlers

Many Vikings sailed to new places, went raiding, and then headed for home. Sometimes, however, Viking people sailed to new places and settled there.

Viking raiders knew that England was wealthy and had good, green land for farming. In the year 865, an army of 3,000 Viking warriors invaded England. The invaders wanted more than just treasure and slaves. This time, the Vikings wanted something they'd never taken before—land!

For more than 20 years, the Vikings battled with England's **Anglo-Saxon** kings and their people. Eventually, the Vikings' invasion was successful and they won a large area of England. This area became known as the Danelaw. Many Vikings settled in England. In time, some even married Anglo-Saxons.

When the Viking language blended with the Anglo-Saxon language, it gave us many English words we use today.

Anger	Gift	Egg
Happy	Run	Sky
Trust	Shake	Reindeer
	Ugly	

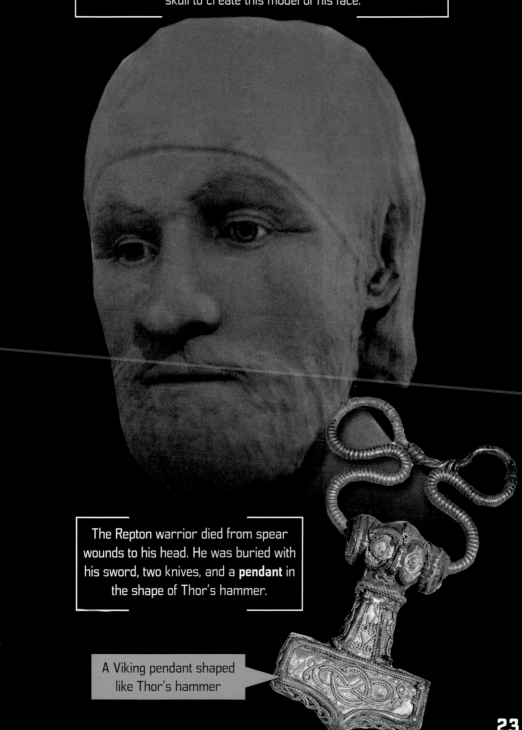

The skeleton of a Viking invader was found buried in the English town of Repton. Scientists used the warrior's skull to create this model of his face.

The Repton warrior died from spear wounds to his head. He was buried with his sword, two knives, and a **pendant** in the shape of Thor's hammer.

A Viking pendant shaped like Thor's hammer

Viking Traders

Many Vikings fought and killed to get their hands on stolen riches.

Not all Vikings were ruthless bandits, however. Some Vikings found more peaceful ways to do business and grow wealthy. They filled their ships with beautiful animal furs and valuable amber. Then they sailed off along rivers through Russia. Along the way, they sold their goods. Some Vikings even stayed in Russia and built new settlements.

Viking traders even visited the great trading city of Constantinople. In the busy markets, Viking furs, amber, and sometimes slaves were sold for silver. They could also be exchanged for silks, spices, and other luxury items from Asia. The Viking traders then sailed home loaded with new and **exotic** goods. They sold these goods to wealthy Vikings.

Vikings collected chunks of amber on beaches. It was used to make jewelry and other decorative objects.

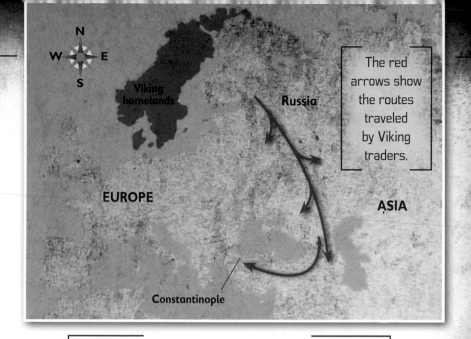

N W E S

Viking homelands

Russia

EUROPE

ASIA

The red arrows show the routes traveled by Viking traders.

Constantinople

Today, Constantinople is called Istanbul. It is the largest city in Turkey. It is home to markets that sell colorful, exotic goods—just like in Viking times!

Viking Explorers

The Vikings' spirit of adventure led them to explore and settle far from their homeland.

Vikings from Norway braved wild and dangerous seas to reach Iceland in the late 800s. Life in cold, empty, rocky Iceland was tough, but so were Viking people. They settled around the coast. They raised animals, caught fish, and hunted for seals, walruses, and whales.

A replica of a Viking stone house in Iceland

A piece of rotten shark

A favorite food of Icelandic Vikings was raw, rotten shark. Chunks of shark meat were buried in sand and allowed to rot. Then they were air dried. People in Iceland still eat this traditional Viking food today.

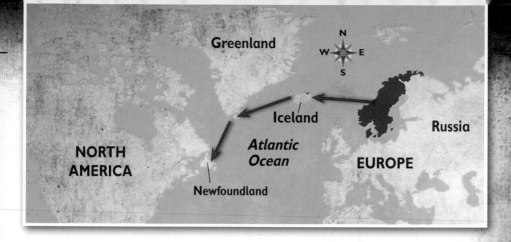

In the year 1000, a fleet of 25 Viking ships set sail from Iceland. They were led by a Viking named Erik the Red. The explorers reached Greenland and built settlements there.

Erik the Red's son Leif Erikson was also an explorer. He sailed to Newfoundland, in modern-day Canada. He may even have explored other places on the east coast of North America. The Vikings did not settle in North America, however.

This painting shows Leif Erikson catching sight of North America.

Into the Afterlife

A Viking warrior spent his life fighting, raiding, and exploring. When the time came, he faced death without fear.

The objects that a Viking man or woman might need in the afterlife were buried with the body. An important or wealthy Viking might be buried with a ship. The body was laid on the ship's deck. Then it was surrounded by clothes, jewelry, money, food, and drink. The Viking's hunting dogs and even horses were sacrificed and laid in the ship. Then the Viking and all the grave goods were buried inside a large mound of soil.

A warrior was buried with his sword at his side. Then he could spend all eternity doing battle in Valhalla.

The Oseberg ship is a Viking longship that was discovered in a burial mound in Norway. The ship was buried in the year 820.

The body of a Viking warrior was carried to Valhalla by warrior goddesses called Valkyries.

Two female bodies were found aboard the Oseberg ship. One woman died in her 80s. It's believed she may have been a Viking queen. The younger woman may have been her slave.

Glossary

ancestor (AN-sess-tur)
A relative who lived a long time ago.
For example, your great-grandparents and
great-great-grandparents are your ancestors.

Anglo-Saxon (AYN-gloh-SAK-suhn)
Belonging to or having to do with a group of
people who lived in Britain from the 400s onward.
They originally migrated to Britain from Germany,
Denmark, and the Netherlands.

exotic (eg-ZAH-tik)
Exciting, unusual, and from a foreign country.

fjord (FYORD)
A long, deep waterway that leads from the sea into
the land. A fjord has high cliffs on each side.

hardy (HAR-dee)
Strong, healthy, and able to survive difficult
conditions, such as extremely cold weather.

merchant (MUR-chuhnt)
A person, usually from history, who buys and sells
goods. Merchants often traveled from place to place
to do business.

monastery (MON-uh-stair-ee)
A building or small settlement where monks, nuns, and other religious people live and worship. In the past, people gave money and valuable gifts to monasteries. The monks often helped people in their local community.

navigate (NAV-uh-gate)
To plan and then guide the direction that a ship, or other vehicle, takes from one place to another.

pendant (PEN-duhnt)
A piece of jewelry that hangs from a chain or cord around the neck.

reputation (rep-yoo-TAY-shuhn)
A belief about someone that is believed by many people and is based on a particular kind of behavior. For example, a warrior's reputation as a hero would be based on his brave actions in battle.

Index

Read More

Margeson, Susan. *Viking
(DK Eyewitness Books).* New York:
DK Publishing (2009).

Phillips, Dee. *Viking: The Story of
a Raider (Yesterday's Voices).* Costa
Mesa, CA: Saddleback Educational
Publishing (2015).

Learn More Online

To learn more about Vikings, go to
www.rubytuesdaybooks.com/viking